ASIAN AIRPOWER

Osprey Colour Series

ASIAN AIRPOWER
— EXOTIC WARPLANES IN ACTION —

PETER STEINEMANN

Published in 1989 by Osprey Publishing Limited
59 Grosvenor Street, London W1X 9DA

© Peter Steinemann 1989

British Library Cataloguing in Publication Data
Steinemann, Peter
    Asian airpower: exotic warbirds in action.
    1. Asian military forces. Military aircraft
    I. Title
    623.74´6´095

ISBN 0—85045—907—9

Editor Dennis Baldry
Designed by Paul Kime
Printed in Hong Kong

Front cover Three generations of jet fighters currently in service with the Pakistan Air Force: a Shenyang F-6 (MiG-19SF) from the fifties; a Mirage 5PA from the sixties; led by an F-16A Fighting Falcon from the seventies. The F-6 and Mirage 5PA belong to the Combat Command School, and the F-16A serves with No 11 'Arrows' Sqn

Back cover Although no longer in front-line service with the Japan Air Self Defence Force (JASDF), the Lockheed F-104J Starfighter is still utilized by the Test Pilots' School. Mitsubishi assembled or manufactured 207 F-104Js (based almost entirely on the F-104C), and 19 F-104DJ two-seat conversion trainers. This immaculate F-104J is test-running its J79-GE-7 turbojet prior to a mission from Gifu Air Base

Title pages Previously equipped with North American F-86F-40 Sabres, Japan's formation aerobatic team 'Blue Impulse' converted to the Mitsubishi T-2 supersonic trainer in 1982. At first sight a *doppelgänger* of the SEPECAT Jaguar T.2 (a similarity extending to the use of license-built Rolls-Royce/Turboméca Adour turbofans), the Mitsubishi aircraft actually differs greatly in detail and is clearly of totally independent design. The Sabre was a hard act to follow, but the team's T-2s perform an immaculate display—including scorching solo runs at low level

Right The author after a photo-flight, in front of a Pakistan Air Force Shenyang FT-6 from No 19 'Sherdils' Air Superiority Sqn at Marsoor Air Base. This was one of the 'comfortable' flights in the Chinese jet, as this particular aircraft is equipped with Martin-Baker PKD10 zero-zero ejection seats

Born in Basle, Switzerland, the author's interest in military aviation became noticeable at a very early age. The European airshow circuit held a magical attraction and he spent most of his free time with a camera visiting various aviation events across Europe.

Always interested in the East, he travelled extensively across Asia and fell in love with the continent, its culture, its people—and its air forces. To be in touch with the East, aviation photographer Peter Steinemann now resides in Melbourne, Australia, from where he still makes many trips to his beloved continent.

Over the years, he has had the opportunity to visit air forces across Asia and many of his pictures have been featured in the international aviation press. In the light of his coverage of Asian airpower, the idea emerged to combine the best of his pictures in this book.

Asian Airpower wouldn't have been possible without the generous help of many people across Asia. Unfortunately, lack of space makes it impossible to mention everyone who assisted, but the author would like to record his sincere thanks to all officers and air crews for the generous hospitality and support which they extended, and for providing photographic facilities. The views expressed in this book are those of the author and do not necessarily reflect those of the air forces covered in *Asian Airpower*.

The photographs in *Asian Airpower* were taken between late 1985 and early 1988 with a Canon A-1 SLR camera and Canon lenses 35–70 mm, 80–200 mm and 300 mm, using Kodachrome 64 film.

Asia does offer a great variation—in people, culture, scenery and climate across the continent—and so does the Asian airpower! Hardware in use is from all over the globe, from the west and the east, from local manufacturers—and in many cases used by the same air force peacefully together.

A lot of the equipment is up to date with the speeding technology in military aviation, but some has been in use for many years and in many cases is already 'vintage' compared with European/American standards. Because of financial limitations and less rapid re-armament in the region, the updating will progress slowly and therefore most of the dated equipment will still give excellent service for some time to the air forces across Asia, but the day for its replacement is not too far away.

Right All the Tiger II sub-types in one formation. Royal Malaysian Air Force F-5E and RF-5E TigerEye from No 12 Sqn, at 30,000 feet in an excellent line-abreast turn

Contents

The Middle East

The *Al Quwwat al-Jawwiya Almalakiya al-Urduniya*—better known in English as Royal Jordanian Air Force (RJAF), has a strength of 7500 personnel and approximately 100 tactical fixed-wing combat aircraft in use, which form eight front-line squadrons. The two main combat types are the Mirage F.1 and F-5E Tiger II

Left A pair of Mirage F.1CJs from No 25 Sqn, based at Ashaheed Mwaffaq as-Salti Air Base flying near Ajlun. The type is able to carry the Matra Super 530F radar homing air-to-air missile (AAM)

Below Their pale grey finish distinguishes the F.1CJs very clearly from the later Mirage F.1EJs from No 1 Sqn, one of which is photographed on the ramp at Ashaheed Mwaffaq as-Salti Air Base—the major RJAF combat airfield

The Northrop F-5E Tiger II is the major RJAF combat type, being utilized by three squadrons. Most of the RJAF's F-5Es are compatible with the Hughes AGM-65D Imaging-IR Maverick missile

Preceding page These two F-5E Tiger IIs from No 9 Sqn carry a pair of AIM-9J Sidewinder AAMs on their wingtips and fly once more for the camera near Ajlun

Right The squadron is based at Prince Hassan Air Base, which is, like most RJAF airfields, located in middle of the desert. Some of the RJAF F-5Es and Fs are kept in natural metal and grey finish

Below This F-5 crewroom certainly has the typical look of the region

The three squadrons from Training Command are attached to the King Hussein Air College and based at Mafraq Air Base. Pilot training to the completion of advanced instruction occupies some 250 hours over a 26-month period

Below These two white T-37Bs carry birthday greetings for HM King Hussein bin Talal of the Hashemite Kingdom of Jordon across their wings!

Preceding pages The first 70 hours are flown on the 20 BAe Bulldog 125s from No 2 Sqn, which makes the RJAF the largest user of this primary trainer outside the UK. The pilot training syllabus includes 110 hours on the Cessna T-37B from No 11 Sqn flown in 104 sorties during a seven-month period. Earlier aircraft were in natural metal finish, those from the second batch still bear the USAF training white

Below Those pilots converted to the rotary-wing fly the Hughes 500D from No 5 Sqn for five months. Not until they have some 500 hours of rotary-wing experience are they considered operationally qualified

The RJAF general-purpose helicopter is the Sikorsky S-76A, 18 of which were delivered to No 7 Sqn based at King Abdullah Air Base near Amman. The delivery included two in the markings of the Red Crescent (the Islamic equivalent of the Red Cross)

These pages Flying north of Amman, this No 7 Sqn Sikorsky S-76A displays the standard three-tone camouflage of the RJAF transport and attack helicopters

The latest additions to the combat force are 24 Bell Cobras. These Cobras are basically modernized AH-1Ss, equipped with a nose-mounted M197 three-barrel 20 mm cannon plus eight HOT launch tubes for the Hughes BGM-71A TOW wire-guided anti-tank missiles. Two squadrons, No 10 and No 12, are equipped with this type and based at King Abdullah Air Base

Left Three Bell Cobra drivers from No 12 Sqn show their flying skills in a three-ship formation over the Amra area. Of course this formation has no tactical use and is purely for the camera

Below This single Bell Cobra shows the extreme manoeuvrability of the modernized AH-1S

Qatar is a small but oil-rich emirate in the centre of the Arabian Gulf. The Qatar Emiri Air Force (QEAF) was established in 1974, mostly with British equipment (Whirlwind, Lynx, Commando and Hunter), but by the early eighties, France took over the position of major weapons supplier with the delivery of Alpha Jets and Mirage F.1s

Preceding page Two Alpha Jet Es and one Mirage F.1EDA from the QEAF in a mixed echelon formation low over the Qatari desert. The 1st Fighter Wing commands No 7 Air Superiority Sqn equipped with 12 Mirage F.1EDAs plus two DA double seaters and No 11 Close Support Sqn equipped with six Alpha Jet Es

Above All QEAF Mirage F.1EDAs are equipped to carry the Matra R.550 Magic AAM as shown on this picture, where the clean lines of the Mirage F.1 are clearly represented

Above The QEAF Alpha Jet E, identified by its dorsal fin extention, is mainly used in the advanced training and light attack role. Pilot training is supplied in Qatar and abroad. The students experience their first flying hours on light aircraft from the Qatar Flying Centre. After graduation from the Centre, the pilots receive their basic flying training in Saudi Arabia on the BAe Strikemaster Mk 80 at the King Faisal Air Academy. Advanced Flying Training is held for six months in the UK on BAe Hawks or on Northrop F-5Fs with the RJAF

Overleaf Flight Lieutenant Sheikh Mohammed Bin Nasser al-Thani from No 11 Close Support Sqn after a very successful photo-flight at Doha Air Base during a hot and humid summer afternoon with temperatures close to 50°C. It certainly changed my perspective about hot weather forever!

The 2nd Rotary Wing commands three helicopter squadrons. One of these is No 6 Close Support Sqn flying 12 SA.342 Gazelles equipped with four HOT launch tubes for the Euromissile wire-guided anti-tank missiles

Above and inset overleaf The camouflage of the QEAF Gazelle blends extremely well into the environment of the desert country. This is extremely important in the case of an anti-tank mission

Overleaf To safeguard their own tanks is one of No 6 Close Support Sqn's missions as shown here—well, in 'close support' with a platoon of Qatar Emiri Army AMX-30S battle-tanks in the desert north of Doha

Mixed echelon formation of two Alpha Jet Es
and a Mirage F.1EDA over the deep blue Inland
Sea in northern Qatar

Above Two Commando Mk 3s are shown with one frigate and three gunboats from the Qatar Emiri Navy in the Arabian Gulf. They carry one AM.39 Exocet each on the left side only

Right Two of the Commando Mk 3s from No 8 ASV Sqn are equipped to carry the history-making AM.39 Exocet. The sea skimming anti-ship missile has proved its deadly efficiency in many conflicts. With a range of between 50 and 70 km, depending on the aircraft's speed at launch, the AM.39 can be fired from well outside a ship's defensive system coverage. The AM.39 has been fitted to a wide variety of aircraft including helicopters and is cleared for firing from Super Frelon, Super Puma and Sea King/Commando. Iraq, Qatar and Pakistan all use this missile

No 8 Anti Surface Vessel Sqn equipped with eight Westland Commando Mk 3s and No 9 Multi Role Sqn equipped with one VIP Westland Commando Mk 2C and three Commando Mk 2Bs are the remaining two helicopter squadrons from the 2nd Rotary Wing

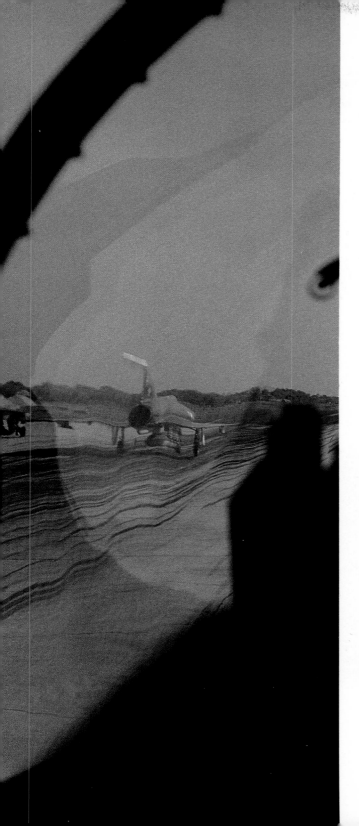

West Asia

The Pakistan Air Force (PAF) is one of the very few which combines front-line warplanes of modern design from China, France and the USA. It is again one of the few whose F-16s actually got involved in air combat against Soviet aircraft. Due to this fact and Pakistan's history, the PAF is Asia's airpower with actual fighting experience gained in two wars against India and during the Soviet intervention in Afghanistan. Once more the famous trio of Chinese, French and US jets—Shenyang F-6 and Mirage 5PA from the Combat Command School (CCS) and GD F-16A from No 11 'Arrows' Sqn on take-off from Sargodha Air Base and in flight over the Swat Hills near the base

Re-equipment of the Shenyang F-6 squadrons that have been the spearhead of the Air Defence Command for many years, started in January 1983 with delivery of the first GD F-16A/B to No 11 'Arrows' Sqn at Sargodha Air Base, which now comprises the Operational Conversion Unit (OCU) for the Fighting Falcon. The second unit converted to F-16 was No 9 Sqn, also based at Sargodha Air Base

The equipment for the 40 PAF F-16s includes ALQ-131 ECM pods, the ALR-69 radar-warning receiver in addition to the AIM-9L Sidewinder AAM, of which four are carried on most patrol flights. Armament provision includes Thomson-CSF ATLIS laser designator pods. The PAF's F-16s were the first non-French aircraft to be equipped with ATLIS

Two F-16s from No 11 'Arrows' Sqn are captured over the Salt Ranges with the Himalayas in the background. The PAF F-16s have the same colour scheme as the USAF and NATO F-16s, including the fashionable grey roundels

This classic shot of the F-16 shows the improvement in view the PAF pilots experienced compared to the F-6, due to the extremely low F-16 canopy frame. However, many F-16 novices (including myself) feel a bit uncomfortable during the first flight because of the undisturbed view. The McDonnell Douglas ACES II zero-zero ejection seat is inclined to 30° and the heel line is raised, which enables the pilot to sustain high G forces—welcome in the 9G club

Above A 60° climb is the maximum climb angle for the F-16 in operational formation for safety reasons. But I can assure everyone that the aircraft is capable of much more in solo flight

Above right The armed F-16s are checked once more by the ground crew before take-off and the pilot keeps his hands clearly visible during this routine—just in case he has a finger near the famous red button

Below right GD F-16B from No 11 'Arrows' Sqn touching down at Sargodha's runway

As the USA halted the supply of hardware after the first Indian war in 1965, the PAF turned to France for the procurement of new high-performance fighters in the form of Mach 2 Dassault Mirage IIIs and 5s for multi role strike, interception and reconnaissance duties. These now equip five or six PAF squadrons

Above One of the latest Mirage 5 models supplied to the PAF is the 5PA3 version in use by No 8 Sqn at Marsoor Air Base. These last Mirages are more advanced and incorporate a Thomson-CSF Cyrano IV fire-control radar for air-to-air and air-to-ground roles and the Thomson-CSF Agave attack radar for use in conjunction with AM.39 Exocet anti-ship missile

Above right Non-radar equipped Mirage 5PAs from the CCS in a clean line-abreast formation north of Sargodha Air Base. The PAF's Mirage fleet is equipped with Matra R.530 and R.550 Magic AAM

Below right Based at Marsoor Air Base, No 22 OCU is the training unit for the Mirage squadrons and is equipped with a variety of Mirage 5PAs, IIIDPs and 5DPs as shown here on an instrument landing approach flown by the converting pilot to Marsoor Air Base over Karachi's suburbs

For many years, major military assistance has been received from the People's Republic of China, starting with the supply of the Shenyang F-6, the Chinese-built MiG-19SF. The F-6 is powered by two Wopen-6s, the Shenyang copy of the Soviet Tumansky R-9BF-811 axial-flow turbojet with afterburner. In PAF service, the F-6 has been developed into an effective Mach 1.4 air superiority and ground attack aircraft, with the installation of some Western avionics and equipment like the Martin-Baker PKD10 zero-zero ejection seat plus the integration of the AIM-9B/J Sidewinder AAM. As a result, the F-6 has been the mainstay of Pakistan's airpower, being used by four or five front-line squadrons

Above The CCS at Sargodha Air Base is unique in that it is the only PAF unit to operate the F-6 in addition to the Mirage 5PA. An elite unit, the CCS can be compared with the USN Fighter Weapons School or the USAF Air Defence Weapons Centre, although it is much smaller

Right It is interesting to see some of the CCS F-6s in the same grey camouflage finish as the F-16, as opposed to the standard F-6 grey finish

Breakaway of three No 15 'Cobra' Sqn F-6s. The unit is based at Peshawar, which is most likely the world's only air base where the runway is crossed by a railway—used twice a week! The centre F-6 is the OC's aircraft, which explains the red and white checks on air intake and fin

Main picture Squadron Leader Safdar from No 19 'Sherdils' Air Superiority Sqn did an excellent job in piloting his F-6 for cannon and rocket firing into the Marsoor firing range. The F-6 is equipped with three NR-30 30 mm cannon, one in each wing root and one under the right side of the nose, but can only fire two at the same time for stability reasons, in this case the fuselage and right wing cannon

Inset Back at Marsoor Air Base, care was taken by the armourers to ensure that no rounds were left in the cannon

The Shenyang FT-5 is a Chinese-developed two-seat version of the MiG-17 and is based on the two-seat MiG-15UTI. The powerplant is a Klimov VK-1 centrifugal turbojet, designated TJ-5D and derived from the Rolls-Royce Nene. The FT-5 remains subsonic with a speed of around Mach 0.92 and an engine overhaul life of 200 hours

Left All PAF pilots undertake fighter training at No1 Fighter Conversion Unit (FCU) at Mianwali, where 102 sorties are flown over 75 hours

Above Training includes basic weaponry: the FT-5 is equipped with a single 23 mm Nudelman-Richter cannon under the nose for air-to-ground gunnery and a radar-ranging sight through a di-electric antenna in a radome above the intake

The whole Shenyang-family in one picture! FT-5 in silver finish from No 1 FCU, FT-6 from No 25 OCU, F-6 from No 14 OCU and a second FT-5 in grey finish, also from No 1 FCU. The Shenyang FT-6 fuselage is an F-6 fuselage lengthened by 84 cm. To make up for the loss of fuel capacity resulting from adding the second cockpit, extra tankage had to be provided in place of the two massive NR-30 wing-root cannons. This allows a safe average training sortie of about 45 minutes, which is about the standard flying time for the Shenyang F-6/FT-6

Top The 'Black Spiders' are one of the three PAF A-5C *Fantan* squadrons and are based at Peshawar Air Base, the oldest military airfield in West Asia dating back to the early twenties—at that time used by the RAF

Above The PAF flies the A-5C in two different colour schemes, sand-green-grey and sand-green-brown. This aircraft, formerly with No 26 'Black Spiders' Sqn, carries one practice bomb on the inner wing pylon.

Left Three A-5Cs from the same squadron represent the latter colour scheme and are seen flying a neat belly-turn near the famous Khyber Pass. The outer pylon is normally used for AIM-9B/J Sidewinder AAM

Developed from the F-6—the air intake is moved from the nose to the wing roots to gain room for a future nose radar—the Nanchang A-5C is a dedicated ground-attack aircraft. Although restricted to strictly visual roles, the A-5C is mostly equipped with Western avionics and Martin-Baker PKD10 zero/zero ejection seat, providing Pakistan with the numerical tactical jet strength at minimum cost

Top The 'Bandits' are the second *Fantan* unit equipped with A-5Cs and based at Marsoor Air Base

Above In spite of the midday heat, I couldn't resist taking a squadron picture of all flying officers together with one of the rare A-5s

Right Low-level flying is a major task for No 7 'Bandits' Tactical Attack Sqn which is incorporated in most training missions

Unique in the PAF is No 2 'Composite' Sqn at Marsoor Air Base, which operates a mixture of vintage US aircraft on target facilities and support duties. They include the last few Martin B-57B/C Canberras, which played an active part in the 1965 and 1971 wars with India

Left The PAF's B-57s are surely the world's last airworthy examples of this type and these pictures show most likely one of the last flights of this classic jet-bomber, which was excellently flown at low level over Karachi Bay by Sqn Ldr Tayyab

Above The Lockheed T-33A and RT-33A are the second type with No 2 'Composite' Squadron and used mainly for target-towing and non-combat tactical reconnaissance. The T-33 was originally in use for advanced jet training before being replaced by the FT-5 in the mid seventies

Main picture Four red T-37Bs from the Basic Flying Training Wing form the PAF's aerobatic team, the 'Sherdils' (lion heart). The aircraft are flown by instructors from the PAF University, here in a two-ship formation over green northern Pakistan

Inset For flying training, the PAF has its own School, College, Academy and now University— 'the home of air warriors', as Risalpur Air Base is called. Primary flying training is 44 hours on the Kamra-built MFI-17B Mushshak with an average dual-to-solo time of 15–17 hours, while a further 120 hours of the basic syllabus are flown on the Cessna T-37B/C jet trainer

Transport support for the PAF is provided by a force of Lockheed C-130B and C-130E Hercules

Left No 6 Tactical Transport Squadron at Chaklala Air Base flies the Hercules in at least four different finishes to cover the various climate-zones across Pakistan

Above This Antonov An-26 represents a transport aircraft with an interesting past. The aircraft was originally delivered to the Afghan Republican Air Force and flown to Pakistan in 1987 by a deserting Afghan crew. The An-26 is now in full PAF markings, but due to lack of spares is rarely flown

South East Asia

Tentera Udara Diraja Malaysia (TUDM) is native Bahasa Malay, but is better known as the Royal Malaysian Air Force (RMAF) elsewhere. A large modernization programme was completed in the mid eighties, which allowed the RMAF to update the flight training syllabus and to expand the front-line squadrons from one to four

Left The Northrop F-5E Tiger II is used widely across Asia, but the RMAF is one of the very few Air Forces which has all sub-types in use— F-5E, RF-5E TigerEye and F-5F are all with No 12 Sqn, the OCU for the RMAF Tiger II

Below A belly shot of one of the RMAF's two RF-5E TigerEyes in a vertical climb shows the nose-mounted camera locations

NO 12

TACTICAL FIGHTER SQUADRON

BEWARE OF TIGERS
CHECK SIX

Main picture No 12 Sqn F-5E Tiger II and RF-5E TigerEye together with a No 11 Sqn F-5F Tiger II in a belly-turn at 30,000 feet high atop the heavy monsoon clouds show the two basic colour schemes, natural finish and two-tone grey, in use with the RMAF Tigers. Due to the rather small size of Malaysia, the F-5's are mostly flown in a clean air superiority configuration

without external fuel tanks and with two AIM-9B Sidewinder AAMs on the wingtips

Inset and overleaf The two RMAF Tiger II squadrons are both based at Butterworth Air Base, which has the typical picturesque environment nicely visible in the background of the F-5F taxying—yes, palm trees

Left The RMAF Skyhawks are remanufactured from ex-USN A-4C and A-4L stock and newly designated as A-4PTM (peculiar to Malaysia). All have been retrofitted with a Lear Siegler AHARS, Ferranti sight and the Hughes Angle Rate Bombing System and can be armed with the AIM-9B Sidewinder AAM, while 20 of the single-seaters are wired for the AGM-65 Maverick air-to-ground missile

Above Clearly shown in this picture are the two camouflage finishes of RMAF Skyhawks

Main picture Originally delivered in the USAF camouflage pattern brown-olive-green, most of the No 9 Sqn Skyhawks are now repainted in a new olive-green finish unique to the RMAF and surely better suited to the flash-green tropics

Inset No 6 Sqn has all six TA-4PTM dual-seaters in use as the unit operates as Skyhawk OCU and is based at Kuantan Air Base together with No 9 Sqn, the second Skyhawk unit

TUDM
M32-17

Advanced jet training is flown on the 12 Aermacchi MB.339As from the No 3 Flying Training Centre (FTC) also based at Kuantan Air Base. No 3 FTC is the first unit where the pilots experience aerial weaponry training—first on a few flights with Pilatus PC-7s equipped with rocket-pods to get the feeling for it, and after on the MB.339A, which is capable of carrying two 30 mm DEFA553 gun-pods and two LAU-3 rocket launchers

Main picture An aircraft in this configuration is illustrated on a rocket firing run at the Kuantan firing range

Insets As this line-abreast formation proves, the instructors from No 3 FTC are indeed the best of the best!

Above The flying syllabus on the Pilatus PC-7 from No 1 Flying Training School at Alor Setar Air Base covers a period of 14 months, with a total of 83 hours of basic training over a four-month period, followed by a similar period in which 97 hours of applied flying instruction are given, whereby the students receive an introduction to instrument and formation flying. After completing the 180-hour flying curriculum to attain their 'wings', the pilots are streamed in accordance with their assessed aptitudes to fast jet, helicopter or transport training

Above right The sun is very strong near the equator and any shade is always welcome, as seen by this PC-7 under repair at Alor Setar Air Base

Below right The RMAF aerobatic team 'Tamin Sari' was formed by instructors assigned to No 1 FTS at Alor Setar Air Base in 1985 and nine PC-7s in a great colour scheme are flown by the team. The team is named after the magic sword of the legendary Hang Tuah, who ruled the Malaysian Peninsula in the 15th century

The topography and distance between the states of the Malaysian Federation implies the need for a fixed-wing air transport element and the DHC-4A Caribou was the RMAF's first aircraft for logistic support. It is still going strong with two squadrons, in spite of the problems with spares which occur from time to time. During the last 22 years, the Caribou has proved outstandingly effective, frequently being called upon to support the ground forces against a background of difficult flying conditions—the Malaysian climate is notoriously unstable and is liable to be affected by heavy and unpredicted storms.

The Caribou's two P&W R-2000 engines make an impressive sight—and sound—from head on, as this Caribou flies low over the hills south of Kuala Lumpur, the home Base for No 1 Sqn

Above As Malaysia is split by the South China Sea into west and east, maritime surveillance is of vital importance. But for many years there wasn't a suitable aircraft available. This changed in 1980, when No 4 Sqn received three Lockheed C-130H-MP Hercules—MP for Maritime Patrol. The starboard door of these C-130s is completely glazed, with an additional bubble window for observation work—which of course is ideal for in-flight photography. To identify foreign vessels, low-level flying is often necessary and to fly in a Hercules at 100 feet over the sea is indeed a special experience

Above right No 2 Sqn, which is based at Kuala Lumpur Air Base, is primarily concerned with government transportation and communications tasks. The squadron possesses a mixed fleet of two Fokker F.28 Fellowship 1000s, two HS.125-400Bs—this aircraft having been named Merpati (Pigeon) in Bahasa Malay, two Canadair CL600 Challengers and a dozen Cessna 402Bs of which one is shown here on a photo-flight near Kuala Lumpur

Below right Two refurbished ex-RCAF Grumman HU-16B Albatrosses joined No 2 Squadron in late 1985 to supply the many islands along the coast of East Malaysia. M35-01 is painted in a tactical two-tone grey finish and M35-02 in a blue colour scheme. The latter aircraft, shown here, is mostly flown in VIP configuration

From its earliest years, the RMAF has given high priority to the creation of a helicopter component and has, for much of its existence, operated a substantial rotary-wing force divided between four squadrons and the helicopter training establishment at Keluang Air Base

Above Each squadron operates a mixture of SA.316B Alouette III and Sikorsky S-61A-4 helicopters, the latter being known somewhat inappropriately in Bahasa Malay as the Nuri, a very small jungle bird! The Alouette III is the longest serving of any RMAF aircraft, fulfilling a variety of tasks, including Forward Air Control (FAC) helicopter, a mission flown by No 3 Sqn from Butterworth Air Base, directing air and ground operations along the Malaysia-Thai border

Left Several Alouette IIIs are maintained on permanent standby for possible border operations and can be flown with a side-door firing machine gun in a gunship configuration. The larger S-61A-4 Nuri is capable of lifting up to 28 troops or 2250 kg of freight on short-range operations. The Nuri rapidly demonstrated its worth in support of counter-insurgency operations. To land a large helicopter like the Nuri in jungle clearings is not an easy task and requires extremely good coordination with a crew member checking the side clearance of the trees to the rotor 85

Compared with most Asian air forces, the Royal Hong Kong Auxiliary Air Force (RHKAAF) is very small, has no combat units and is actually a department of the Hong Kong Government operating out of Hong Kong's Kai Tak International Airport. Manned by close to 100 full-time government employees and around 150 volunteers, its principal roles are coastal patrol, anti-smuggling duties, SAR and survey work. As would be expected, aircraft play an important role in a territory made up of 236 islands and much mountainous terrain. It is therefore not surprising that the helicopter takes a major share in performing these roles. More than 100 helipads make up for the shortage of conventional runways and underline the importance of helicopters

Above The RHKAAF has its hangar and control centre on the east side at Kai Tak International airport, very close to the water with a large apron which offers enough space to accommodate all the RHKAAF's aircraft at once

Right Three SA.365C Dauphins make up the Force's spearhead. They are usually flown single-pilot with an observer on the shorter daytime missions. Two-pilot operation is standard by night or on long-duration flights. For the night roles, a search light is usually carried. Other items of equipment include a loud hailer, long-range tanks, detachable winches and safety floats in case of emergency landing on water

Above The RHKAAF fixed-wing fleet is made up of two BAe Bulldog 128s, one BN-2A Islander and one Cessna 404 Titan. The Bulldogs are mostly used in the basic flying training role, but will be soon replaced by four Slingsby T.67M-200 Fireflies. In this process, the pilots and crewmen are examined by an RAF examining unit and are tested and categorized to RAF standards. The Bulldog HKG-6 is flown here by the first woman in training with the RHKAAF

Right The Islander was acquired in 1972, followed by the single Cessna 404 Titan in 1979. Both 'twins' operate on long-range or long-endurance missions for aerial surveys, long-range search and rescue and off-shore surveillance

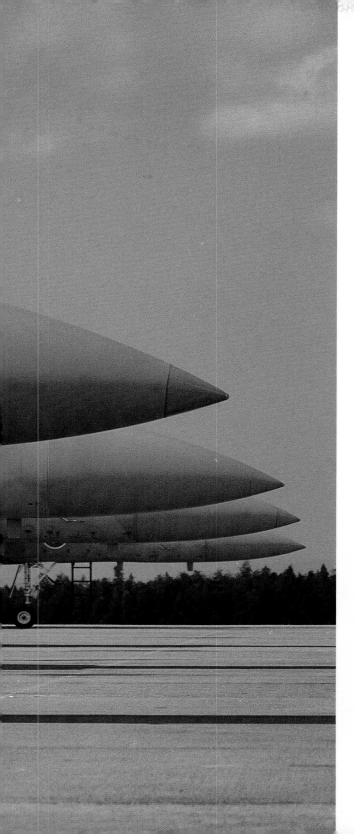

The Far East

The *Koku Jieitai*, which reads in English Japan Air Self Defence Force (JASDF) is primarily a fighter-equipped defence force, as there is no strike force nor in-flight refuelling capability. Front-line equipment is operated by 14 squadrons assigned to interceptor, support fighter and tactical reconnaissance duties. Despite Japan's negligible defence spending of just 1% of the GNP, the JASDF combat

squadrons are well equipped with modern hardware like F-15Js, F-4EFs and F-1s, which makes the JASDF one of the best equipped air powers in the Far East

Preceding pages The McDonnell Douglas F-15J Eagle is firmly established as the prime JASDF combat aircraft already equipping six squadrons. With the exception of a few sensitive components, such as ECM and radar-warning equipment, the F-15's technology has been transferred across the Pacific for licensed manufacture by a Mitsubishi-led group of aerospace companies, including IHI for the P&W F100 turbofans. The group is also producing the AIM-9L Sidewinder and AIM-7E Sparrow AAMs for the F-15J in Japan. The 204th *Hikotai* at Hyakuri Air Base, 100 km north of Tokyo, was one of the first Eagle units. An average of 20 to 30 sorties are flown each day, during which the pilots often encounter Soviet aircraft such as *Bears*, *Cubs* and *Badgers*

These pages F-15J from the 202nd *Hikotai* on touch-down at Nyutabaru Air Base with the massive airbrake extended

Inset The squadron marking is a 'Bujin Haniwa', which is a clay image of a warrior and was excavated from an ancient Kofun tomb, one of which is near Nyutabaru Air Base. The Eagle entered JASDF service in December 1981 with the Rinji F-15 *Hikotai* (Temporary F-15 Sqn) at Nyutabaru Air Base on Kyushu for pilot training. Retaining this OCU role, the unit became redesignated as 202nd *Hikotai* in December 1982, taking the title of a former F-104 squadron from the same base

Left and far left A plum flower is the marking for the 305th *Hikotai* based at Hyakuri Air Base. Their McDonnell Douglas F-4EJ Phantoms are still a key component in Japan's air defence and will serve together with the Eagles well into the next decade, as the result of a service-life extension programme (SLEP), which began in 1987 and includes AN/APG-66J pulse-Doppler radar, an advanced fire-control system, head-up display (HUD) and inertial navigation system

Below The Japanese have a very different attitude towards comic books and magazines from people in the west, and they are extremely popular. This doesn't stop at the Air Base gate, as is illustrated on this FOD (Foreign Object Damage) warning sign at Hyakuri Air Base

A Phantom from the 304th *Hikotai* after take-off from Tsuiki Air Base on Kyushu. An old tale says that a long nosed goblin lives on Mount Ehiko near Tsuiki Air Base, and the 304th *Hikotai* selected the 'Tengu' mask as their unit marking

These pages and overleaf The 501st *Hikotai* at
Hyakuri Air Base is the JASDF's only dedicated
reconnaissance unit, which will continue to
operate the 14 US-built RF-4EJ recce Phantoms
received in the mid-seventies for some time.
Due to the nature of the operations flown by the
501st *Hikotai*, their Phantoms are camouflaged
in green-olive-tan for low-level flying.

Below After each flight, the crew has to fill out several forms and hand the aircraft over to the ground crew to prepare it for the next task

Left Misawa Air Base is the home of the Mitsubishi F-1s of the 3rd *Hikotai*, the first squadron of which converted to the F-1s during 1978. They proudly display a Samurai helmet as squadron marking on the fin. The F-1 is actually a development from the Mitsubishi T-2 dual-seat trainer. The airframe is still the same, but the space for the second occupant is used for extra fuel and electronic equipment. The F-1 is a fighter-bomber armed with Mitsubishi ASM-1 anti-ship missiles, which is assigned to surface attack of any seaborne invasion. But because of Japan's 'Defence Force' status, the F-1 is described there as a 'support fighter' armed with 'anti-landing craft' missiles! Three *Hikotais* fly nearly 80 F-1s, which were the first JASDF aircraft to standardize on the green-olive-tan camouflage scheme. Like the Phantom, the F-1 will undergo a SLEP to extend its life into the mid nineties, when the FS-X programme will be well on the way to replacing the F-1 with the improved Japanese F-16

Above Some of the *Hiko Kyodotai's* T-2s have shaded-off nose, fin and wing leading edges, which leaves the remaining grey areas of the aircraft looking very similar to a MiG-21 silhouette. The T-2 Koki model is equipped with an internal 20 mm Vulcan rotary cannon, although most T-2s from the training command are unarmed T-2 Zenki trainers

Inset overleaf The *Hiko Kyodotai* is Japan's equivalent to an Aggressor Squadron

Overleaf Based at Nyutabaru Air Base, their Mitsubishi T-2 Kokis are finished in several shades of grey paint with a Soviet Air Force look-alike number on the nose

The 'Blue Impulse' aerobatic team re-equipped with the T-2 within the 21st *Hikotai* in early 1982 and their eight aircraft are based at Matsushima Air Base. Of interest is the fact that the Blue Impulse colour scheme was created through a nationwide school competition and the winner was a 15-year-old girl

With its only 'overseas' commitments being operations between Japan's islands, the JASDF requires only a small transport force. Yuso Kokudan is the Air Transport Wing and comprises the 401st, 402nd and 403rd Hikotais, which are equipped with a mixture of Kawasaki C-1s, NAMC YS-11s and since March 1984 with Lockheed C-130H Hercules

Left The 401st *Hikotai* at Komaki Air Base has so far received six of the 12 Hercules on order, of which the first four are painted in Lizard (European II) camouflage and the last two in the Vietnam camouflage scheme. Some 29 of the 31 Kawasaki C-1s originally delivered remain with the three transport *Hikotais*, after two were lost in a catastrophic double hill-strike in formation during April 1983. Since then, progress is under way to equip the C-1 with anti-collision radar

Above The C-1 has STOL capability as demonstrated by this C-1 from the 402nd *Hikotai* based at Iruma Air Base. The bird marking on the fin stylizes the number 2 for the 2nd *Yuso Kokutai*, by which the 402nd *Hikotai* is controlled

The Kawasaki C-1ECM is certainly not the best looking airframe and still under development with the APW at Gifu Air Base

With over 300 aircraft, the Japan Maritime Self Defence Force (JMSDF) air element comprises some 12,000 personnel assigned principally to ASW and general maritime patrol operations, with mine-sweeping a further task of importance. Although only a few helicopters go to sea on ships platforms, organization is on lines similar to the USN. The 121st *Kokutai* is already equipped with the new HSS-2B and based at Tateyama Air Base. Three additional *Kokutais* form the 21st *Kogugun*, the principal HSS-2 operator. All Mitsubishi Sikorsky S-61AHs so far built have been issued to the SAR flights across Japan. Each *Kogugun* has one *Kyunan Hikotai* (SAR flight) and this S-61AH belongs to the *Kyunan Hikotai* from the 2nd *Kogugun* based at Hachinohe Air Base—all indeed a little bit complicated. The Sikorsky Sea King—still known by its pre-1962 USN designation HSS-2, contributes substantially to the JMSDF's anti-submarine operation. The Mitsubishi licence-built HSS-2 is sonar-equipped and has been in production since 1964, but the latest model, the HSS-2B, is a considerable advance on its forebears, having sonar, search radar and ESM equipment

Above The JMSDF is currently in the throes of a major re-equipment programme for its fixed-wing patrol fleet, following the selection of the Lockheed P-3C Orion as a replacement for the Kawasaki-built Lockheed P-2J Neptunes. The latter will remain in service into the early nineties and is still flown by three *Kokutais*. The major difference to the P-2H is the replacement of the piston engine with GE T64 turboprops. The Neptunes from the 3rd *Kokutai* at Atsugi Air Base are already history, as the unit converted to the Orion during 1985

Left The 51st *Kokutai*, which is the naval service trials unit, is based also at Atsugi and flies Orions, Neptunes, and HSS-2s. One of their Neptunes is ready for take-off on Atsugi's runway

Overleaf This P-2J from the 3rd *Kokutai* with feathered starboard prop makes an emergency landing at Atsugi after an engine failure. But, thanks to its two J3-IHI-7C auxiliary turbojets, the situation is not too critical

JMSDF Orions entered operational service in March 1983 and the type is now the JMSDF's principal ASW patrol aircraft. The Orion's armament includes McDonnell Douglas AGM-84 Harpoon anti-ship missiles and the indigenous GRX-3 homing torpedo. An Orion from the 6th *Kokutai* shortly before touch-down at Atsugi's runway. It was the first Orion unit, formed in March 1983 to introduce the new type into squadron service

海上自衛隊

Above Only after washing does the eight person crew disembark. Note the Japanese *Kanshi* for JMSDF on the fuselage

Far left As one of the few navies to operate flying boats and amphibians in an operational role, the JMSDF assigns Shin Meiwa PS-1 to the 31st *Kokutai* at Iwakuni Air Base. Fitted with 'dunking' sonar for deployment after alighting on the surface of the sea, the first PS-1 entered service in 1968 and only 14 of the 23 received remain in operation. The PS-1 is not an amphibian, as the wheels in the hull are only for beaching

Left Back on base, the first thing is to clean the aircraft of sea-water and for this purpose, a special 'washing-street' is installed at Iwakuni Air Base

To see the PS-1 take off and land is indeed an experience, but to see the flying boat perform in rough seas on a stormy day is something else. In these conditions, the crew's flying skill is severely tested

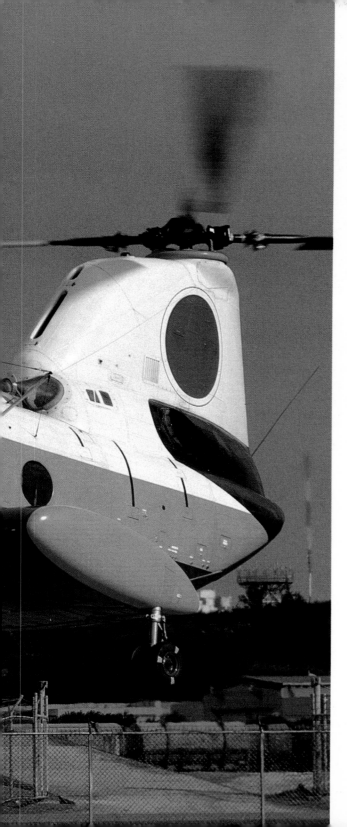

The Japan Ground Self Defence Force has over 400 aircraft, comprising 25 fixed-wing and nearly 400 helicopters including Bell AH-1J tactical support helicopters. These aircraft are assigned to 24 squadrons attached to five geographical armies, together with an independent helicopter brigade and a training group

These pages and overleaf Under the *Seibu Homen Kokutai* (Western Army Air Group) is the 1st *Konseidan* (Composite Brigade) and its sole component, the 101st *Hikotai*, is the most colourful of the JGSDF *Hikotais*. The reason for the bright white-orange-olive colour scheme of the unit's Mitsubishi LR-1s (overleaf), Bell UH-1H Iroquois (above) and Kawasaki-Vertol KV-107s (left) is the fact that the unit is based at Naha Air Base on the island of Okinawa—if they are forced to ditch, their bright plumage is a significant aid to prompt location and rescue

127